WHEN I'm SAD

Written and illustrated
by
JANE AARON

Golden Books
NEW YORK

Golden Books®
888 Seventh Avenue
New York, NY 10106

Copyright © 1998 by Jane Aaron
All rights reserved, including the right of reproduction
in whole or in part in any form.
Golden Books® and colophon are trademarks of
Golden Books Publishing Co., Inc.

Designed by Gwen Petruska Gürkan

Manufactured in the United States of America

10 9 8 7 6 5 4 3 2 1

Library of Congress Cataloging-in-Publication Data

Aaron, Jane.
    When I'm sad / written and illustrated by Jane Aaron.
        p.   cm.— (The language of parenting)
    Summary: Explains sadness as a normal part of life and discusses how to deal with it.
Includes a parents' guide with examples and suggestions.
    ISBN 0-307-44058-3 (alk. paper)
    1. Sadness in children—Juvenile literature. 2. Parenting. 3. Child rearing.
[1. Sadness.] I. Title. II. Series.
BF723.S15A37 1998
152.4—dc21   98-36330
                                                      CIP
                                                      AC

For Nana

Sometimes
I feel
SAD

MY MOM says, "CHEER UP"

My DAD tries to make ME LAUGH

but I just feel SAD

Sometimes I feel sad when my mom has to go away

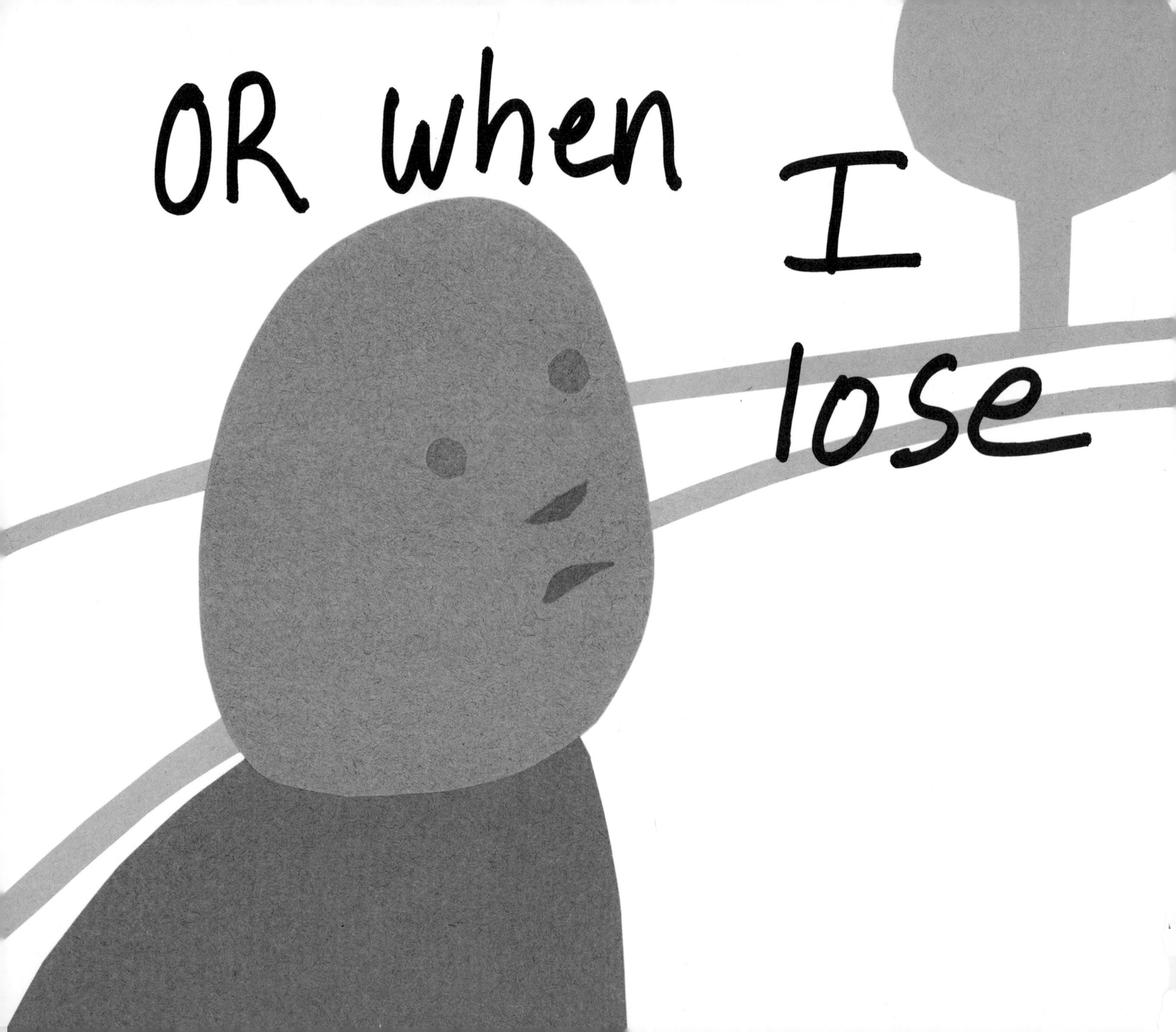
OR when I lose

one
of my
toys

I feel
sad
when
my parents

yell at me

or at each other

when
I'm sad

I don't feel like playing

and
I don't
feel
like talking

SOMETIMES EVEN WHEN I DON'T HAVE TEARS

I STILL FEEL LIKE I'm CRYING

MY DAD SAYS it's OKAY TO CRY

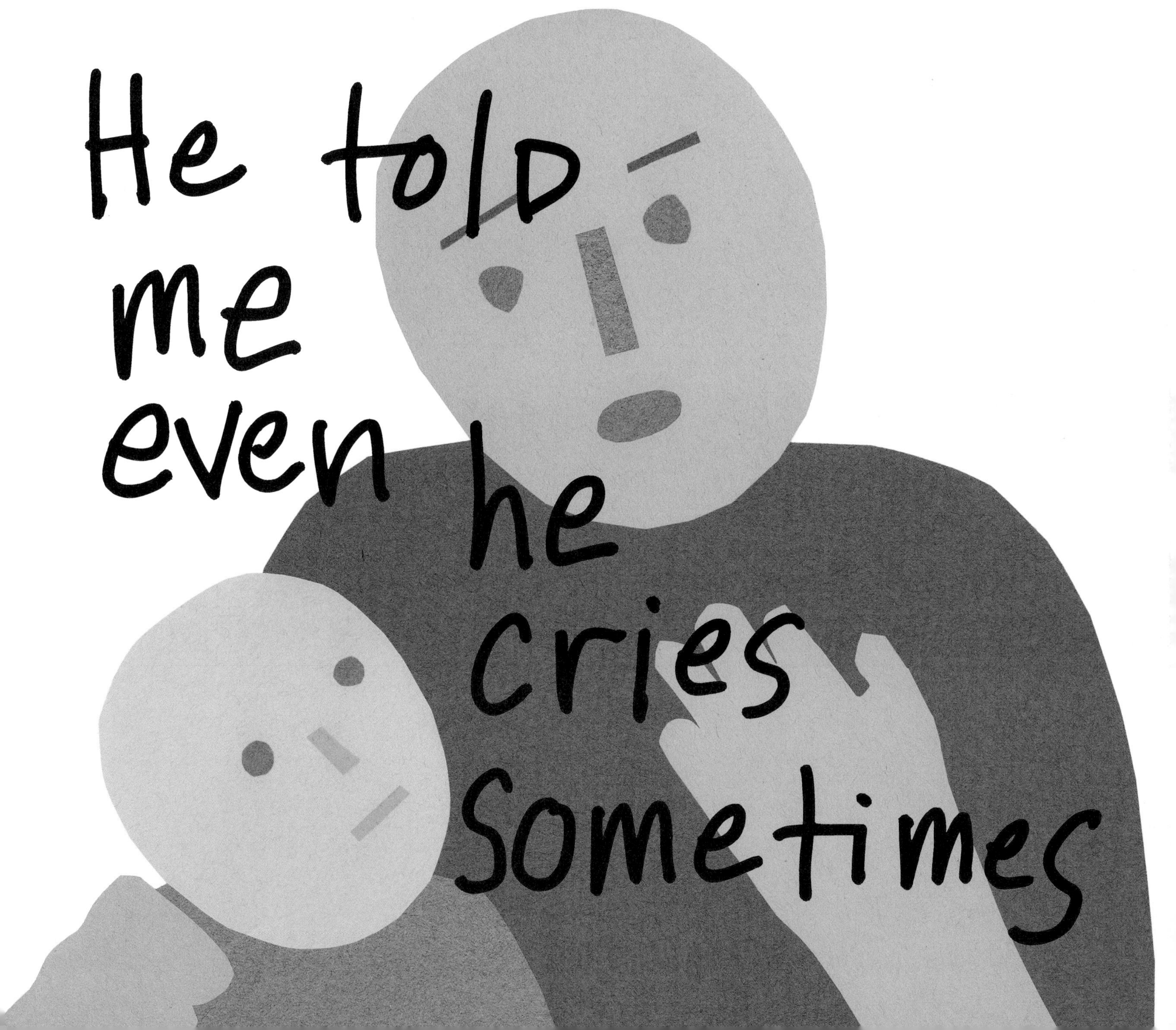
He told me even he cries sometimes

when I
feel sad
I like
being CUDDLED

or playing

with

my toys

Sometimes I like to draw pictures

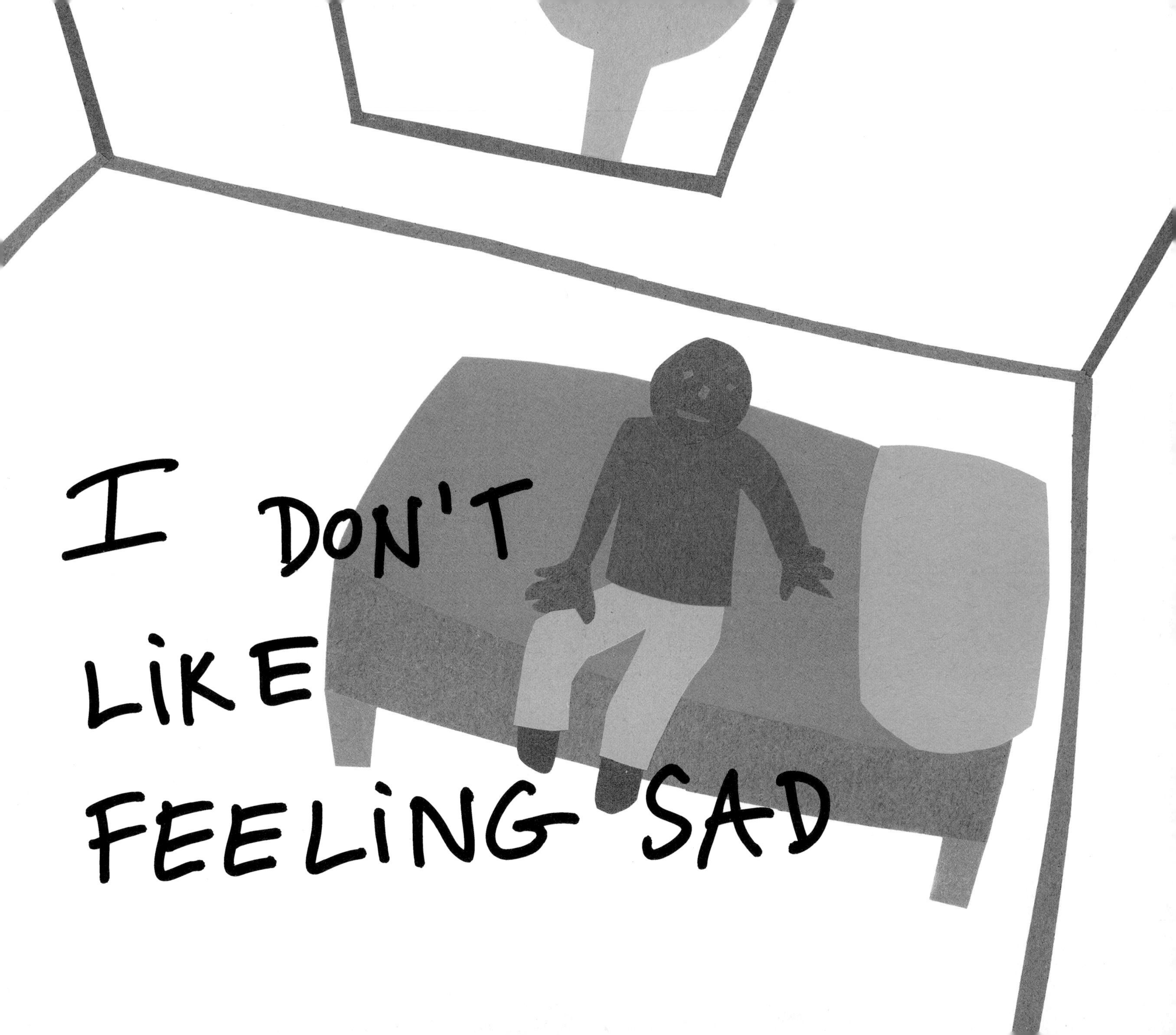
I DON'T
LIKE
FEELING SAD

but
I'm
happy that
it never
lasts too long